Reforming the Income Tax System

Reforming the Income Tax System

William E. Simon

American Enterprise Institute for Public Policy Research
Washington and London

William E. Simon, secretary of the Treasury from 1974 to 1977 and author of *A Time for Truth,* is a financial consultant in New York City.

Library of Congress Cataloging in Publication Data

Simon, William E., 1927–
Reforming the income tax system.

(Studies in tax policy) (AEI studies ; 319)
1. Income tax—United States. I. Title. II. Series. III. Series: AEI studies ; 319.
HJ4652.S474 336.24'15'0973 81–3475
ISBN 0–8447–3437–3 AACR2

AEI Studies 319

Printed in the United States of America

Contents

PREFACE vii

1 INTRODUCTION 1

U.S. Economic Strength Deteriorates 1
The Focus of This Study 4
The Growing Tax Reform Movement 9

2 THE PURPOSES OF THE TAX SYSTEM: PAST AND PRESENT 13

Early History of the Tax System 13
Loopholes 14
Macroeconomic Tax Policy 16

3 OBJECTIVES OF REFORM 19

Economic Efficiency 20
Simplicity 23
Horizontal Equity 24
Progressivity 25

4 PROPOSALS TO REFORM THE TAX SYSTEM 33

Comprehensive Income Base 34
Consumption or Cash-Flow Tax 37

5 THE EXPERIENCES OF OTHER INDUSTRIAL NATIONS 43

6 A FINAL NOTE 47

APPENDIX 49

List of Tables

1. Personal Savings in Six Industrialized Nations, 1977 3
2. Nonresidential Fixed Investment in Six Industrialized Nations, 1966–1976 3
3. Average Annual Rate of Increase of Output per Hour in Manufacturing, 1960–1976 4
4. Total Government Expenditures as a Percentage of Gross National Product and of National Income, 1950–1979 5

Preface

A complete overhaul of the U.S. tax system is long overdue. In December 1975, in a speech to the Tax Foundation, I called for a return to the basic principles upon which our income tax system was founded—equity, efficiency, and simplicity. I said that we need to wipe the slate clean of personal tax preferences, special deductions and credits, exclusions from income, and the like and impose a single, simple progressive tax on all individuals. I felt that I was speaking for millions of Americans who were fed up with the present tax system and wanted it replaced with one they could understand and trust. In the years that have passed since that speech, I have received overwhelming evidence that this is indeed the way the American people feel.

Soon after my 1975 speech I initiated a comprehensive study of basic tax reform at the Treasury Department. The goal of that study was to develop tax policy alternatives that were based on clear and consistent principles. The end product had to be a system which looked as though it was designed on purpose, so that it could be understood by every taxpayer.

We began by examining the concept of "income" and what it should mean as a base for federal taxation. We were aiming at an ideal concept, but recognized that some compromises and modifications were necessary to keep the system simple and politically practical.

The report, known as *Blueprints for Basic Tax Reform*, developed two specific model tax systems.[1] The first broadens the base of

[1] Department of the Treasury, *Blueprints for Basic Tax Reform*, 1977.

the income tax. It calls for the integration of the corporate income and personal income taxes, the taxation of capital gains at full rates after adjustments for inflation, and the taxation of many other items that presently are not taxed.

The second model uses consumption as the basis of the tax system. It is called a cash-flow tax, and because our current system possesses many similarities to this model, it would not be as radical as it may seem at first sight. Savings are excluded from taxation, but are taxed fully if withdrawn to finance consumption. As shown in the *Blueprints,* the tax can be progressive and although I do not believe that the tax structure should be used to redistribute economic well-being, I recognize that political compromise is necessary on this issue. With a broadly based definition of consumption, a three-bracket system with rates from 10 to 40 percent could raise the same amount of revenue as is raised currently while having only modest effects on the distribution of the tax burden.

After years of attempting piecemeal reform, I am convinced that a fundamental reform is necessary. We can no longer afford to tinker. We must design an entirely new system and adopt it as an integrated whole. Either of the models outlined in the *Blueprints* is vastly superior to the present system. Each has a broader tax base and lower and simpler tax rates. I prefer the cash-flow concept because it would contribute more to an increased rate of capital formation, which is so badly needed by our nation. But the comprehensive income tax system would also enhance the efficiency of the economy by reducing the extent to which economic decisions were based mainly on the desire to exploit tax loopholes.

This monograph restates the basic case for tax reform and explains the alternatives in less technical language than was used in the *Blueprints*. For the technical reader an appendix provides more detail.

Although this work focuses on tax reform, it is written at a time when the spending side of the budget is out of control. Indeed, the state of our spending laws, especially those related to entitlements, is as terrifying as the state of our tax laws. Clearly, it will be extraordinarily difficult to reform the tax side of our system in a sensible way unless we find some way to constrain the explosion in spending. That must be done so that we can more easily go on to adopt the fundamental tax reforms described in the following chapters.

Independent research institutions are very helpful in stimulating the dialogue that can lead to sensible tax reform. For that reason, I was delighted when the American Enterprise Institute asked me to chair the advisory council for its tax policy studies program. The institute has since produced many research studies and has held several conferences designed to clarify the nature of the tax system. I would like to give special thanks to Ronald Utt, who assisted in the preparation of this manuscript, and to the AEI staff, which aided in its completion. I am especially grateful to Rudolph Penner, who provided valuable assistance at every stage of the development of the analysis, and to Isabel Davidov, who typed the many, many drafts.

1
Introduction

American economic history may have reached a turning point in the 1970s. It was a decade distinguished by an unpredictable but continual inflation, a lackluster growth in worker productivity, a steep decline in the international value of the dollar, and a minimal gain in our standard of living. The statistics clearly confirm these trends. The reality of these cold facts is reflected in the "malaise" that has recently been a topic of public concern and in the uncertainty with which we deal with other nations and with our domestic problems.

U.S. Economic Strength Deteriorates

Consider, in contrast, our relative economic position in the world during the preceding two decades. In the 1950s and 1960s, our standard of living advanced at a rapid rate and was well above that of the other industrialized nations. Our currency was strong and in demand. The dollar became the preferred medium of exchange in international transactions. Foreign central banks held it willingly as an important reserve asset. American workers and managers, known for their productivity, inventiveness, and management skills, still seemed to be pulling away from the rest of the world in innovation and product development.

In the late 1960s, J. J. Servan-Schreiber, French author and publisher, wrote a book titled *The American Challenge,* documenting these impressive gains and calling for Europeans to change their attitudes and business practices or they would be completely overwhelmed by the awesome productivity of the American economic machine. In one of the early chapters of the book, Servan-Schreiber vividly described the challenge facing Europeans:

> What threatens to crush us today is not a torrent of riches, but a more intelligent use of skills. While French, German or Italian firms are still groping around in the new open spaces provided by the Treaty of Rome, afraid to emerge from the dilapidated shelter of their old habits, American industry has gauged the terrain and is now rolling from Naples to Amsterdam with the ease and speed of Israeli tanks in the Sinai desert.[2]

No one would write such a book in the 1980s. Although our standard of living is still among the highest of the industrialized nations, other nations have narrowed the gap and do not share our chronic problems of low productivity growth, meager investment, and generally unstable economic conditions. Embarrassing signs of this disorder are starting to emerge: the dollar is no longer one of the strong currencies; our trade negotiators flock to the East in search of concessions; and, in the politest of terms, our European friends are now gently advising us to change our ways. The *Economist* of London wrote, a few years ago, that "America is set for industrial senility unless its industrial investment goes from a British rate to a Franco-German rate."[3]

What has happened in the past decade or two to account for this near reversal of roles? The view is emerging that, as a nation, we are no longer building for the future. Consider, for example, some important measures of our aggregate economic behavior.

Table 1 shows our personal savings rate, the proportion of current income that we set aside for the future to be invested in productive capital. It is the lowest of the major industrialized countries.

Not surprisingly, capital investment per country reflects the same trend. U.S. investment in productive capital, as a percentage of gross domestic production, has also been the lowest of the industrialized countries, as shown in table 2.

[2] Jean-Jacques Servan-Schreiber, *The American Challenge* (New York: Atheneum, 1968), p. 29.
[3] *Economist*, February 28, 1976, p. 21.

TABLE 1

PERSONAL SAVINGS IN SIX INDUSTRIALIZED NATIONS, 1977
(percentage of after-tax income)

Country	*Average Personal Savings*
Japan	21.5
France	16.1
West Germany	14.0
United Kingdom	13.9
Canada	9.8
United States	5.1

SOURCE: Organization for Economic Cooperation and Development.

TABLE 2

NONRESIDENTIAL FIXED INVESTMENT IN SIX INDUSTRIALIZED NATIONS, 1966–1976
(percentage of real gross domestic product)

Country	*Average Investment*
Japan	26.4
West Germany	17.4
Canada	17.2
France	16.7
United Kingdom	14.9
United States	13.5

SOURCE: Executive Office of the President, *Economic Report of the President, 1979*, p. 125, table 28.

In research and development, an American strength for many years, signs of slippage may be seen. The percentage of gross national product we spend on research and development declined from 3 percent in 1963 to 2.3 percent by 1974.[4] In 1973, West Germany edged past the United States in the proportion of gross national product devoted to science and engineering.

What do these trends imply for our standard of living? When investment is depressed, the growth of productive capacity ob-

[4] William E. Simon, "The Role of Private Investment in the U.S. and the World," ICC speech in Orlando, October 2, 1978, p. 6.

TABLE 3

AVERAGE ANNUAL RATE OF INCREASE OF OUTPUT PER HOUR IN MANUFACTURING, 1960–1976

(percent)

Country	*1960–1976*	*1960–1966*	*1966–1976*
Japan	8.5	8.8	8.4
Netherlands	7.0	5.6	7.8
Belgium	6.9	5.0	8.1
Denmark	6.7	5.4	7.5
Italy	5.8	6.7	5.3
Sweden	5.7	6.5	5.2
West Germany	5.6	5.6	5.7
France	5.6	5.5	5.7
Canada	3.9	4.3	3.6
United Kingdom	3.3	3.7	3.0
United States	2.9	4.0	2.2

SOURCE: U.S. Department of Labor, Bureau of Labor Statistics, *Handbook of Labor Statistics, 1978,* June 1979, p. 582, and calculations.

viously declines. Obsolete capital is replaced at a slower rate, and the productivity of the work force either declines or grows more slowly than we have come to expect. In addition, the economy fails to develop the new technologies that enhance production and expand output.

As table 3 illustrates, U.S. productivity not only lags behind that of the other industrial countries but also has worsened considerably over the past several years. Over the ten years ending in 1976, our rate of increase in productivity was only one-fourth that of the Japanese and not quite three-fourths that of the United Kingdom, a country often cited as being in an advanced state of economic decay.

With growth in output per worker diminished, gains in our standard of living are reduced accordingly. Our consumption is nothing more than the fruits of our own and of others' labor. With less produced, there is less to go around.

The Focus of this Study

A multitude of factors account for our economic decline in relation to what others are achieving, what we have achieved, and, sadly,

TABLE 4

TOTAL GOVERNMENT EXPENDITURES AS A PERCENTAGE OF GROSS NATIONAL PRODUCT AND OF NATIONAL INCOME, 1950–1979

Year	*Percent of GNP*	*Percent of National Income*
1950	21.3	25.8
1955	24.5	29.9
1960	27.0	33.1
1965	27.3	33.2
1970	31.7	39.1
1975	34.9	43.9
1977	33.0	41.0
1979	32.0	39.4

SOURCE: Council of Economic Advisers, *Economic Report of the President*, January 1980, pp. 222, 288.

what we could achieve. Some of the more frequently mentioned reasons include the decline in innovation and initiative; the preference for more leisure rather than work; the rapid growth of a stultifying layer of government regulations; the misallocation of the share of our wealth that flows in growing volumes to the public sector; and, the subject of this book, the tax system. It is a system that encourages consumption more than saving and discourages investment and enterprise by placing increasingly burdensome rates of taxation on the gains accruing from such endeavors.

The last two reasons cannot be separated as independent factors (indeed, all five are interdependent) because the rapid growth in government expenditures has had to be funded by rising taxes. Increasingly these funds have had to come from the middle- and upper-income taxpayers who are responsible for most of this nation's savings and investment. Table 4 illustrates the rising claim of the three levels of government on America's income. In the past three decades, total expenditures by all levels of government have increased from one-fifth of our gross national product to nearly one-third and from about one-quarter of national income to about 40 percent.

About 90 percent of personal income tax collections come from households in the top half of the income distribution. The burden of funding the government's escalating expenditures falls heavily on our more productive citizens, who contribute the most to our economic growth through their savings and investment, as well as their entrepreneurial, professional, and scientific skills. With taxes taking ever-increasing shares of a person's income, concern is now being expressed that such levels of taxation are having an adverse impact upon work effort. One need not possess an advanced degree in economics to realize that if government taxes an activity heavily enough, people will refrain from engaging in that activity.

The matter is worsened by inflation. Since 1977, various federal personal income tax cuts have not offset the fact that, as nominal incomes are raised by inflation, taxpayers find themselves pushed into higher and higher tax brackets. This so-called bracket creep has proceeded so rapidly that a vast majority of taxpayers now pay a higher tax on each additional dollar of income than they did before the Kennedy-Johnson tax cut of 1964–1965. That large cut in marginal tax rates was hailed for its contribution to economic efficiency. Except in the highest and lowest tax brackets that contribution has largely been destroyed by inflation.

Bracket creep is bad enough, but inflation's effect on the taxation of capital income is even worse. According to the Department of Commerce, corporations paid taxes on $28.2 billion of fake profits in the third quarter of 1980 because inflation had eroded the real value of the depreciation deductions allowed for tax purposes (those deductions are based on original cost) to a level far below the true worth of the capital stock that is being worn out. In addition, they paid taxes on $35.9 billion of false inventory profits.[5] The two adjustments imply that taxable profits exceed inflation-adjusted profits by one-third, and some would argue that the Department of Commerce depreciation adjustment is insufficient. Corporations gain an offsetting advantage in that the inflated interest rate on their debt is fully deductible even though the real value of the debt that must be repaid is eroded by inflation. But for every borrower who is gaining an advantage, there is a poor lender who typically pays a tax on the inflated interest rate. These two effects roughly offset each other as the income produced by the corporation is passed through to the

[5] Council of Economic Advisers, *Economic Indicators*, December 1980, p. 4.

bondholder who supplied the capital. When equity capital is supplied by savers, they frequently incur a capital gains tax even though a large portion of the increased share value results from inflation and in no way enhances the real purchasing power of the shareholder.

The issue of taxation and its effect on work and investment is a relationship on which economists are focusing more and more attention. To argue that taxation adversely affects work incentives is not necessarily to imply that anyone will therefore refrain from working (though some evidence suggests that personal income taxes in conjunction with generous welfare and unemployment benefits promote this effect at the lower end of the income spectrum).[6] Rather, the potential workers in a family may not be so eager to take advantage of incremental work and investment opportunities. These include extra employment; employment leading to promotions (and higher tax brackets); employment of a spouse at relatively low wages, which will be taxed at the primary worker's top marginal tax bracket; and savings whose returns will be taxed at the margin. When marginal tax rates are high, workers are reluctant to engage in such activities. It just is not worth it. The distortion of these incremental work and investment decisions has a major impact on the long-term health of the economy. It was, after all, our entrepreneurship and the energy to use our abundant natural resources that gave us our high standard of living. When we squelch initiative, we undermine the foundations of our prosperity.

Another focus of this study is the taxation of gains from investment and the impact of these taxes on economic growth and productivity. I have already noted the debilitating impact of inflation on the taxation of capital income. Even without inflation the double taxation of corporate profits, first at the corporate level

[6] See Edward D. Kalacheck and Fredric Q. Raines, "Labor Supply and Lower Income Workers," in *The President's Commission on Income Maintenance Programs* (1970), pp. 159–81; Michael J. Boskin, "The Effects of Taxes on the Supply of Labor: With Special Reference to Income Maintenance Programs," in *Proceedings of the Sixty-Fourth Annual Conference on Taxation*, pp. 684–98, and Boskin, "The Economics of Labor Supply," in Glen G. Cain and Harold W. Watts, eds., *Income Maintenance and Labor Supply* (Chicago: Rand McNally, 1973), pp. 163–81; and Irwin Garfinkle, "On Estimating the Labor Supply Effects of a Negative Income Tax," in Cain and Watts, *Income Maintenance*, pp. 205–64.

and then at the individual level when dividends and capital gains are received by the stockholders, causes grave inefficiencies. With the income stream taxed twice, corporations can invest only in those endeavors that have a high expected return. The shareholders' ultimate, after-tax return, therefore, must merit the risk of potential loss and must be at least comparable to the yields on assets and investments that are not taxed twice. Many productive corporate investments with returns that would be adequate in a more nearly neutral tax environment must be passed over because the expected income will not be great enough to survive the double gauntlet of a corporate tax and personal tax rates as high as 70 percent on capital income. Investment is pushed into less productive sectors that are not taxed twice, and we are a poorer nation as a result.

For the worker, savings are discouraged. The income he allocates to savings and investment is taxed when earned (one must save out of after-tax income); it is taxed again when dividends or interest is paid; and it is taxed finally on any capital gains that may arise on the sale of assets, even if those gains are due entirely to inflation. Had the worker chosen to spend his earnings, his future tax obligation would have been less. Our treatment of individual savings and investment income is in sharp contrast to the preferential tax treatment of such incomes in most other industrialized countries.

Although our treatment of corporate capital income is especially severe, the tax code includes numerous tax breaks to specific kinds of capital income that serve to misallocate our limited investment resources. Preferential treatment of residential housing, income-producing real estate, state and local debt obligations, industrial revenue bonds, and other assets distorts market allocation mechanisms and channels capital resources into less productive endeavors. The generous treatment of pension income, while it tends to reduce the disincentives to total savings, distorts its timing and may, because of the regulatory restraints on pension funds, reduce overall risk taking. All of this is done for the purpose of meeting specific social objectives that might otherwise be neglected. There is, however, little hard evidence to show that such concessions are successful in meeting their goals or that the benefits that follow exceed the costs associated with the misallocation of our scarce capital resources.

These are just a few of the major problems with our tax system. Not only are economic incentives distorted, but also gross inequities are created among households comparably situated in the same income class. Moreoever, the mind-boggling complexity of the system drove 43 percent of the taxpayers in 1977 to seek paid, professional assistance in the preparation of their returns.[7]

The Growing Tax Reform Movement

It is the adverse economic effects of the tax system that have recently given rise to the concern over the inequities and inefficiencies inherent in it and that have spawned a growing reform movement throughout the country. In the past the tax reform movement—both theoretically and politically—was dominated by those whose primary interest was in shifting ever greater amounts of the tax burden to businesses and wealthy persons. Today the converse is true: the most prominent tax reform proponents now are those who emphasize economic efficiency rather than income redistribution and who therefore want desperately to remove those perverse incentives that diminish investment and productivity.

But there is a severe danger that the society is becoming more polarized. At one extreme, a growing proportion of the bottom half of the income distribution has been absolved of paying personal income taxes because of the rapid growth of the standard deductions and the invention of the earned income credit. Many of these people live in congressional districts in central cities, where much of the income comes from government programs. There will, therefore, always be a solid core of congressmen calling for increased tax rates and bigger programs, and with enough logrolling they may often get their way.

On the other side there is a strong grass-roots movement of ordinary citizens who feel overtaxed and overregulated. In California, they rose up in anger and passed Proposition 13, and similar movements have arisen in other states and localities in a more moderate form.

At present, concern for the taxpayer seems to be in the ascendancy, and it is having some impact on political decision mak-

[7] Conversation with officials of the Internal Revenue Service.

ing. The tax reform legislation of 1978 marked the first time since the Vietnam War that tax relief was focused on the upper middle class and capital gains taxation was eased significantly. In fact, concern for the state of our nation's rate of capital investment was a hallmark of the 96th Congress, receiving significant support from diverse segments of both parties. Reflecting this, a recent report of the Joint Economic Committee of Congress supported the need for changes in the tax laws to promote greater amounts of investment.

In effect, this new focus on the debilitating impact of our current tax law follows from a realignment of some of the major social groups. For decades many working Americans have expressed either support for or indifference to the growth in the number of social responsibilities and objectives assumed by government. The support began to erode, however, when it became apparent that the objectives were not being met despite the expenditure of extraordinary sums of money. At the same time government pressed into increasingly trivial areas of concern, with a concomitant increase in the bureaucratization of American life. Together with the rising rate of taxation needed to finance these endeavors, this combination of events led many Americans to question and ultimately to oppose the growing influence of government in their lives. The election of 1980 clearly rejected the type of liberalism which dominated government actions in the late 1960s and early 1970s.

Will this mood continue? Both the public and the Congress that represents them are fickle creatures, and a spurt in unemployment or a few screams of anguish over program cuts could cause voting trends to change at any time.

But any reversal of recent voting trends should at least be slowed down by recently developed analytical and statistical evidence. Several economists have demonstrated the adverse effect that elements of our tax system have on capital formation.[8]

[8] See Michael J. Boskin, "Taxation, Savings, and the Rate of Interest," *Journal of Political Economy*, vol. 86, no. 2, part 2 (April 1978), pp. S3–S27; Martin Feldstein and Lawrence Summers, "Inflation and the Taxation of Capital Income in the Corporate Sector," *National Tax Journal*, vol. 32 (December 1979); and Charles Becker and Don Fullerton, "Income Tax Incentives to Promote Savings," *NBER Working Papers*, no. 487 (June 1980), pp. 4–7.

Younger members of the economics profession have been accumulating impressive evidence as to the system's negative effects. Their work further supports the objective of comprehensive tax reforms that this nation urgently needs if it is to meet the goal of a rapidly rising standard of living.

I welcome these changes and the intent behind the many movements for reform. We must, however, recognize that incremental alterations, changes in percentage rates, and spasmodic cutbacks will not necessarily rationalize the tax system and enable it to raise the desired amount of revenues in an uncomplicated fashion while minimizing economic disincentives.

Achieving this end requires a comprehensive overhaul of the system. Anything short of this, as is the case with most of the proposed reforms to date, would leave the existing problems largely intact. The system would still be complex, inequitable, and hostile to income from capital investment.

This task of comprehensive reform is monumental in its dimensions and far reaching in its potential impact on our economic well-being. It is essential, therefore, that we start at the beginning. We must define the basic purpose of the tax system, consider and evaluate its numerous objectives, and use the revised and restated objectives to build a system that better serves our nation's needs.

Such an approach is not an empty, academic exercise. Our tax system is complex, chaotic, and contradictory for the simple reason that it has been called upon to perform an extraordinarily diverse set of tasks, many of which have in time come into conflict with one another. As each new national objective has arisen, a set of incentives or disincentives has been added to the tax system. Each change is incremental and, by itself, has little effect on the main body of tax law. Cumulatively, however, such alterations add up to enormous complexities, inconsistencies, and unanticipated penalties. This is the situation we find ourselves in now. For this reason, we must start afresh.

Both marginal and average tax rates could be lowered and inefficiencies diminished if government spending could be reduced relative to total production and income. Throughout my career I have been a strong advocate of lower spending levels. But this is a book about tax policy, and it will focus on that side of the budget. This focus on tax policy should certainly not be interpreted as indicating any satisfaction with the amount that government spends.

A given amount of revenue can be raised in a variety of ways. Our marginal tax rates are high not only because government spending is too high, but also because our laws have greatly diminished the proportion of total income subject to taxation. The complex system of preferences, concessions, and credits greatly reduces tax rates on some types of income, but then necessitates high marginal and average tax rates on what is left over. Marginal rates on income are then raised further by our misguided attempts to make the personal income tax highly progressive with respect to the diminished tax base that remains. Any analysis of tax reform must therefore focus on three main questions. First, how can we broaden the tax base to achieve our main goals of simplicity, efficiency, and equity? Second, should the broadened base be taxed progressively? If so, how progressively? Third, should the base to which taxes are applied be income or consumption?

2

The Purposes of the Tax System: Past and Present

Early History of the Tax System

When our government and its activities were small, revenues from tariffs and excises were sufficient to fund government operations. By the early twentieth century, government's assumption of limited social responsibilities increased revenue needs, thereby requiring the implementation of an income tax through the adoption of the Sixteenth Amendment in 1913. America's subsequent entry into World War I added to the financial needs that had to be funded through the income tax. In the 1920s, tax rates were low throughout the income distribution. While government involvement in various new activities had expanded during the first third of the century, total government expenditures came to only 10 percent of gross national product in 1929, and three-quarters of this amount was attributable to state and local government spending.[9]

The expanded social objectives arising from the economic trauma of the 1930s increased the government's perceived need for funds. President Franklin D. Roosevelt's New Deal created a new freedom—freedom from want—and led the government into adopting new spending programs that guaranteed a minimum level of security. But the increase in the government's command over the resources of the society corrupted traditional philosoph-

[9] Executive Office of the President, *Economic Report of the President, 1981*, pp. 233, 318.

ical notions of freedom as our leaders sought a middle ground between pure capitalism and pure socialism. Massive mobilization for World War II added to this, and tax rates rose sharply. As average rates of personal taxation were raised, the system became more steeply progressive, and corporate tax rates were also increased. By and large, the structure of our existing system is the legacy of this era.

With the tax rates on marginal income now very high and with the government assuming greater social responsibilities, the progressive tax system came to be seen as an important tool of wealth redistribution. It took income from well-to-do people and corporations to provide expanded services to low- and moderate-income households. Much of the academic analysis of the tax system concentrated on its income redistribution effects to determine if, in fact, it was fair. Were there too many loopholes that allowed the rich to escape with their wealth intact?

Loopholes

With concern focused on the system's redistributive efficiency, it is easy to overlook the fact that many of these so-called loopholes were intentionally created and preserved. Many special tax provisions attempted to direct capital and entrepreneurial talent toward endeavors deemed to further national objectives. Viewed this way, these tax concessions represent a dimension of the tax system that goes well beyond its basic revenue-raising function: taxes came to be used as penalties and rewards to influence the direction of society's allocation of resources. Tax exemption of the interest on state and local bonds was originally adopted to avoid any possible constitutional problems. Now it clearly exists not only because of constitutional considerations but largely to facilitate public borrowing for capital improvements. Highly preferential treatment for capital gains on owner-occupied housing and the deductibility of mortgage interest expenses remain largely unchallenged because they are believed to facilitate home ownership. Tax credits for insulation, storm windows, and other energy conservation measures were implemented to reduce our dependence on imported oil. Accelerated depreciation and investment tax credits were adopted to encourage capital investment when that objective became important. These exemptions are only a few among many. Although they work to reduce the effective progressivity of the tax system, they do so inefficiently and inequitably. Moreover, these concessions have been adopted over a long period, with little reconsideration in light of changing circumstances. As a consequence, our tax system is so littered with exceptions and preferences that it exceeds the ability of most Americans to file their own tax returns correctly.

A far better mechanism for promoting economic and social objectives is to do so explicity through the expenditure side of the budget. Here such support would be more visible and under closer scrutiny. It could thus be channeled more directly to the targeted areas. To attempt to achieve the same end with the tax system is to adopt a shotgun approach. Benefits flow willy-nilly to those who need them as well as to those who do not. The costs of such tax manipulations, in terms of forgone revenues and misallocated resources, may exceed the value of their benefits.

Yet any politician trying to change things takes his life in his hands. One man's "loophole" is another's divine right. As Senator Russell Long so aptly put it, tax reform has come to mean, "Don't tax you; don't tax me; tax the fellow behind the tree." Furthermore, many of these tax concessions tend to result in some degree in reduced prices for goods and services in a competitive economy. Every proposed change is met with the cry that it will put some taxpayers or some industry out of business.

While many loopholes clearly intend to favor some purpose that some politicians regarded as being "good" at some time in our past history, it is probably also the case that many loopholes would not have arisen were it not for the very high marginal rates which resulted from our misguided attempts to make the tax system highly progressive. With one hand the politicians responded to the egalitarians and created a structure of rapidly rising marginal tax rates. When they saw that this discouraged certain valued activities and generally reduced entrepreneurship, they used their other hand to create loopholes which muted the disincentive effects of the progressive tax structure they had earlier created.

Clearly it would have been better to rethink the whole notion of how progressive the tax rate structure should be. This matter is discussed in great detail later. Here it is only important to note that in their efforts both to please the egalitarians by designing a highly progressive rate structure and to please entrepreneurs by creating a plethora of exemptions to that structure, the politicians have succeeded only in creating an unholy mess. Entrepreneurship, which should be devoted to making economically productive investments, is instead diverted into efforts to gain every last advantage from our Byzantine tax structure.

Macroeconomic Tax Policy

Another major function of the tax system is its periodic use as a tool of macroeconomic stabilization policy. In the 1960s, with the wide acceptance of Keynesian economic principles, policy makers sought to fine-tune the economy by means of tax changes. Many politicians and economists came to view the tax system in aggregate as a major tool to achieve aggregate economic objectives. Across-the-board cuts or increases in taxes, together with the appropriate expenditure targets and monetary policy, have been implemented to stimulate or to retard the economy, depending on whether unemployment or inflation was the problem to be solved.

The success achieved in the early 1960s in using the tax system to stimulate the economy has made proposals for a macroeconomic tax policy strategy a biennial event in Washington. These events are, in part, the essence of the problem as Congress, the executive branch, and a hundred special interest groups wrestle with the system, changing this and adding that, and pushing the tax system in a multitude of directions to attain social and economic objectives. Most often legislators suddenly discover, during election years, that we "need" tax cuts to stimulate the economy. As a result deficits soar and inflation reaches new heights as the monetary authorities are pressured into buying more government debt.

Each legislative initiative to alter the tax system becomes a golden opportunity for various special interest groups. It allows the congressmen, executives, trade associations, and self-appointed public interest groups to seek special consideration for the promotion of some special cause. By complicating the tax system, they prove their worth to their constituents and succeed in the noblest cause of all—perpetuating their own existence. At the broadest point of conflict, lines are drawn between those who would channel relief to people with lower-end incomes in order to achieve both economic stimulation and income redistribution and others who would prefer to see greater gains for the business and investment sector in order to stimulate the economy through increased capital investment.

Many more narrow objectives are added, to further the confusion: special relief for tuition payments, child care, export promotion, pollution control, energy efficiency, inner-city development, and so on, and so on. Smaller pressure groups combine and factions are formed when their objectives are not contradictory. Subcompromises are worked out, some ground is given, and some ground is gained. Major factions then confront each other and, knowing that rigid adherence to principles and goals will lead to an impasse, compromise further. Finally a set of proposals with majority support and presidential approval emerges. Each round of the battle adds to the fray those who have just received special tax concessions and who now must join the fight to hold on to what they have recently gained. Compromise becomes the handmaiden of complexity and moves us even further from the ideal system. That system would be simple to comply with and administer, equitable to all, and reasonably neutral with regard to resource allocation, so as not to interfere with economic growth.

Because our system falls short of this ideal, we find ourselves saddled with a tax system that raises revenue but does so in an increasingly complex way. Complying with and administering the system require an enormous volume of scarce resources, and the system contains enough economic disincentives to have a measurable effect upon the wealth of the nation. More important, it is a system that Americans increasingly disrespect. They see others gaining at their expense, either through tax loopholes for those in income brackets above them or through increasingly generous income transfers for those below. Evidence of this disrespect can be found in the recent estimates of the size of the so-called underground economy, an economy based on cash and barter transactions, all unreported and difficult to trace. From comprehensive audits of sample tax returns, the Internal Revenue Service (IRS) has estimated that unreported individual income in 1976 may have amounted to as much as $100 to $135 billion from legal and illegal sources.[10] Other scholars, such as Gutmann and Feige, have estimated that unreported income is even higher. Gutmann, using data on the demand for currency, estimated that $250 billion of income escaped taxation in 1979, while Feige suggests a number above $500 billion or over one-fifth of GNP.[11] Such studies are much criticized because there is really no good way of getting evidence on tax evasion. But even the modest estimates of the IRS indicate that the system is in real trouble. For some groups, tax evasion has become almost a way of life. The IRS and the Census Bureau estimate that 30 to 52 percent of farmers' income goes unrecorded. The IRS estimates that among the self-employed, such as household domestics, independent contractors, and professionals, only 60 percent of income is reported.[12]

For the average American, the tax system is his day-to-day link with government. When its basic structure is called into question, the foundation of government by consensus is threatened. We are, at heart, a generous and honest people, expecting no more than fair play and basic equity. When these are seen to be little valued by major social institutions, embittered hostility sets in. We see growing signs of this hostility now, directed at taxes. When these feelings are considered in conjunction with the economic malaise now confronting the country, we can see the urgency of the need for comprehensive tax reform.

[10] U.S. Department of the Treasury, Internal Revenue Service, *Estimates of Income Unreported on Individual Income Tax Returns*, 1979, pp. 6–7, table 1, and pp. 16–17, table 4.

[11] Peter M. Gutmann, "The Subterranean Economy," *Financial Analysis Journal*, November-December 1977, p. 26, and testimony of Gutmann to the Joint Economic Committee of the U.S. Congress, November 15, 1979; and Edgar L. Feige, "The Irregular Economy: Its Size and Macroeconomic Implications," Social Systems Research Institute Workshop Series (unpublished paper, University of Wisconsin at Madison, May 1979).

[12] IRS, *Estimates of Income Unreported*, table F–1, footnotes 6 and 10, pp. 96–104; and "The Income Farmers Hide," *Business Week*, April 17, 1978, pp. 91–94.

3
Objectives of Reform

In thinking about the nature of these comprehensive reforms, we must keep in mind the many objectives of our tax system as well as the many problems. Otherwise, we might lose sight of our purpose and diminish our chances of creating something close to the ideal.

A large part of the current problem is that we have asked the tax system to do too much. It is supposed to fund government provision of goods, services, and transfer payments; it is supposed to stabilize the economy; and it must redistribute income. As if this were not enough, it has been complicated beyond reason by efforts to encourage "socially productive" activities, which is often a euphemism for saying that politicians use it to curry favor with narrow interest groups.

As a result of all of this, the tax system does nothing very well and often does outright harm to the people that it is trying to help. The excessively progressive tax system, for example, which was supposed to be beneficial to the poor, reduces work effort and investment and diminishes the amount of income that is left to redistribute. A larger portion of a smaller pie may not be very nutritious. In the United Kingdom, where very high tax rates come into effect at middle-income levels, the per capita standard of living is now only slightly higher than it is in Italy—historically one of the poorest of the Western European countries.

I shall not detail all of the adverse effects associated with attempts to meet varying and often contradictory objectives through tax policy, though careless and irrational adherence to such objectives has surely contributed to some of our current economic problems. I propose the substitution of a new set of objectives to guide our tax reform efforts. These new objectives are economic efficiency; simplicity; equity among those at the same income level (or horizontal equity); and a lesser degree of progressivity that will lessen the work and investment disincentives inherent in the existing system.

Economic Efficiency

I consider economic efficiency to be the most important of the objectives, in part because it facilitates the attainment of the other three objectives. More significantly, it leads to a tax system more conducive to the right amount of savings, investment, and economic growth and to a rising standard of living. To this end, my reform proposals have as their primary goal a tax system capable of raising the required revenues while entailing minimal disincentives to work, to capital formation, and to the efficient allocation of the nation's resources. I recognize, of course, that any practical tax system, regardless of form, will adversely affect incentives by reducing the net gain from productive endeavors. My intention is to reduce these disincentives to an absolute minimum. Suitable reform of the existing system can generally be accomplished by altering the treatment of income and other gains attributable to capital and by moderating the degree of tax rate progressivity. Under current law, such income is taxed several times at excessive rates and often on the illusory gains from inflation.

My reform proposals will achieve greater economic efficiency by making the tax system more neutral in its impact on the savings and consumption decisions of households and on the allocation of their investments among alternative opportunities. The system presently promotes consumption by penalizing savings. The saver cannot be rewarded with the whole return to the capital investment that he finances because the tax system drains some of that return away. Any narrowing of the gap between the rate of return to investment and the reward to savers would lead to greater investment and higher future incomes.

The first goal of economic efficiency is the improvement of the savings/consumption trade-off. The second goal is the promotion of greater efficiency in the allocation of savings and capital among alternative uses. Specifically, the system should be neutral as to the uses to which the funds are put. Unhindered by complicated tax concessions and penalties, and with motivation based wholly on expected profits adjusted for risk, the market system would allow capital to flow where the expected return and productivity are the greatest. Under such an allocative mechanism, total income and production would be higher than they are under our current system, which often encourages scarce capital resources to flow into relatively unproductive uses.

Ironically, our tax system explicitly recognizes the negative impact of existing taxation on capital formation by granting special concessions and privileges to individuals and businesses that engage in certain investment activities. Residential housing and commercial real estate have historically been accorded special treatment to encourage investment in these areas. As a result, we end up with more buildings than we would otherwise have and less of something else—productive plant, equipment, and new technologies. This incentive toward overinvestment in preferential areas is particularly true of owner-occupied residential housing, where capital gains are largely sheltered and where interest payments are deductible, while the return to the housing investment (the elimination of the need to pay rent) goes untaxed. These capital gains privileges are especially important in times of high inflation. There has been a tremendous incentive for people to channel their funds into their dwellings as well as into small-scale rental enterprises to take advantage of tax shelter opportunities. In such an environment, home prices are bid up to excessive levels, and the debt requirement to fund these transactions drains capital away from other sectors of the economy. While making such residential investments, Americans have been net disinvestors of corporate equities in eighteen of the past nineteen years. Of course, inflation has greatly intensified the shift from business to housing capital over the last decade. It creates enormous uncertainty for the business investor and, as previously explained, raises the tax burden on business investment by eroding the value of depreciation deductions, creating false inventory profits, and creating false capital gains on equity. Housing gains a large relative advantage because high nominal mortgage rates are deductible while the real value of the mortgage debt is eroded.

The tax concession to housing and other forms of real estate is only one of many ways that the tax system serves to misallocate capital. The exemption from federal taxes of the interest on state and local debt obligations encourages these governments to invest in projects whose productive returns are scarcely half of the return needed to attract investments in the private sector. The investment tax credit, first implemented in the 1960s to spur capital formation, provides unequal benefits to firms and thus distorts the allocative mechanism. Since it is of direct value only to firms with positive profits and no losses to carry forward, the program has given rise to a whole new field of equipment leasing. This technique enables the tax benefit to be split by the lessee and the lessor when the investing firm cannot directly take advantage of the tax credit because of inadequate profits. These leasing companies provide a useful service facilitating investment in certain activities by reducing the taxation of capital income, but they do so in a roundabout and expensive manner. They require extra operating resources that could be used more productively elsewhere.

Other such special exemptions include energy conservation credits and special depreciation write-offs, which serve to channel funds artificially into certain types of investments at the expense of other, more productive ones. Thus, they serve to misallocate capital in a way that leads to a lower total national income.

The many complex tax concessions for investment in the existing system could be replaced by a tax system that simply *does not discourage* investment. Such a system would achieve the goal of promoting capital formation without the inherent inequity and allocative distortions that now pervade our economy. A system that was more neutral toward investment and, hence, more economically efficient would also facilitate the attainment of other reform objectives. Improvements in horizontal equity and simplicity would be fulfilled because, in effect, a tax system that is neutral toward investment requires the elimination of many of the existing tax preferences. The elimination of these concessions—a closing of the loopholes—will streamline the tax system, thereby promoting simplicity. It will greatly diminish the ability of some persons substantially to shelter portions of their income, thereby promoting horizontal equity.

Simplicity

The objective of simplicity has obvious merits to anyone who has labored to complete a tax return. A tax system that permits a host of special deductions from or adjustments to gross income to determine taxable income requires more resources for record keeping, preparation, and official review than one that has fewer deductions and adjustments. A significant amount of talented human labor is now needed to operate the system from both the paying and the collecting ends. This labor could be used in the production of goods and services that people would choose to purchase. While to some the preparation of a tax return at home is nothing more than an annual nuisance, nearly half the filing households had to avail themselves of the services of a professional to complete their 1977 forms, including an astonishing 40 percent of the persons filing the "simple" form 1040A. Virtually all large business firms have to maintain full-time legal and accounting staffs for this purpose, as well as seek the guidance of independent professionals, usually lawyers and accountants, and expensive ones at that. If this complexity is unnecessary, and I and many others contend that it is, then the mere operation of our present system imposes a deadweight loss on the nation. Any reduction in this complexity would reduce this loss and increase the amount of discretionary income available to businesses and households.

A related issue is that so much human ingenuity is devoted to legal tax avoidance of this incredibly complex system. Even more unfortunate is the effort given to illegal tax evasion because of the difficulty of discovery amid the complexities. The structure of many business firms, their types of transactions, and their choice of economic activity are often chosen on grounds of tax reduction rather than on the basis of pure economic efficiency. Under such circumstances, the choice that is the most profitable for the entrepreneur is not necessarily the one that is of greatest productive benefit to society. In the language of economics, the social return on these activities is less than the private return. In some instances, cattle breeding, oil-well drilling, real estate investment, leasing, and financial intermediation are undertaken primarily to reduce tax burdens. The investor frequently gives far too little attention to whether these investments pay a positive rate of return before taxes. Not only do these endeavors waste tangible resources; they also misdirect entrepreneurial talents, perhaps the most important economic and social resource in a free society.

Horizontal Equity

The objective of horizontal equity would be partially fulfilled by satisfying the first two objectives, because its attainment, too, is contingent upon eliminating many of the exceptions. For tax purposes, horizontal equity means that persons or households earning the same level of income should pay the same amount of taxes. Because there are numerous opportunities for tax shelters for appropriately situated persons, this objective is often not met. In the extreme case, there are the widely publicized examples of persons with substantial incomes paying no taxes or fewer dollars in taxes than does the average wage earner.

While such instances are memorable and often infuriating, they are rare and count for little in the way of the overall tax loss. In 1977, for example, there were fewer than seventy returns that paid no tax out of over 50,000 filed with adjusted gross incomes over $200,000.[13] The average tax paid on such returns was $166,600. What is of significance, though, is the somewhat smaller but more widespread discrepancies that occur among those with more moderate levels of wealth. With so many shelters available, persons with comparable incomes can have markedly different tax obligations, depending on how their income is earned and invested and on how their business activities are structured. A common discrepancy arises in the treatment of renters and of homeowners. Because they can deduct property taxes and interest payments and can shelter capital gains, homeowners pay less in taxes over their lifetime than do renters who invest their savings in stocks, bonds, or savings accounts rather than in houses. They must pay taxes on the returns from such investments.

[13] U.S. Department of the Treasury, Internal Revenue Service, *Individual Income Tax Returns*, 1980, table 1.1, p. 7, and table 1–D, p. 6.

Progressivity

The final objective of my reform is to limit the degree of tax rate progressivity and marginal tax rates, to minimize the creation of work and investment disincentives. I oppose progressive taxation because of the philosophic conviction that people are deserving of the fruits of their labor and the economic judgment that progression wreaks havoc on economic efficiency. A very low flat rate tax on a comprehensive income base could allow a generous basic exemption and still raise sufficient revenues while minimizing disincentives to save and invest. For example, with a $1,000 basic exemption, current income tax receipts could be raised with a flat tax rate slightly less than 14 percent (our current bottom rate) if all personal income were included in the tax base. Although such a low tax rate is obviously desirable for its economic efficiency, any comprehensive reform program must be acceptable to at least a majority of Americans. I recognize that there is in our society a widespread acceptance of the belief that the tax system should incorporate some degree of progressivity. As a consequence, my proposal provides for a progressive rate structure, but one with much lower marginal tax rates than those in our current system.

This concession to facilitate acceptance of comprehensive tax reform does not imply that the issue is of secondary importance. It is of crucial importance, and it merits our close attention, especially in light of the perverse effects that our steeply progressive system, with its high marginal tax rates on middle incomes, creates in an inflationary environment.

Although the income tax has been progressive since its inception, the justifications for progressivity have often changed. After Congress decided it was inappropriate to impose more taxes on very low income groups, it sought a system with some degree of progressivity to raise the revenue required to fund government activities. This was the "practical" justification for the system. It has been morally justified by the concept of "ability to pay," since the rich can more easily afford the necessities of life and have more discretionary income. Progressive rates would achieve the desired revenue without causing undue hardship.

As the issue of equity grew in importance and as the government sought to foster greater equality of wealth among citizens, the progressive tax system became a vehicle for achieving that goal. The technical and moral justification for this approach was based on a misuse of economic theory and of nineteenth-century utilitarian philosophy. In its crudest form, this theory held that an individual's utility—a general measure of his economic well-being—was directly related to his income but that the relationship was characterized by diminishing returns. This means that successive and equal increases in income add successively smaller increments to an individual's total utility. Applied to society as a whole, this concept implied that an extra dollar was of greater value to a person with a low income than to one with a high income. Taking dollars from the rich and giving them to the poor would increase total utility because total net benefits would exceed the losses. The presumed social utility function implied that a progressive tax was an ideal revenue-raising device because it enabled government to collect the required amount of taxes at the least cost to society's well-being.

As broad-based concepts of equality became important national objectives—as evidenced by the legislative trends over the past fifty years—the existence of the progressive tax structure appeared to be increasingly appropriate and desirable. Meanwhile, explicit programs for income redistribution became firmly entrenched as national policies, and they required substantial funding. Progressive taxes thus became more and more important as a revenue-raising device. Indeed, in several of the other industrialized nations committed to extensive social welfare goals, steeply progressive marginal tax rates approach 100 percent on incomes above some socially desired midrange. Many believe that any significant reduction in high rates of this type would create a substantial shortfall in government revenues.

As Milton Friedman has pointed out, however, this view is totally misguided. He notes that in 1977, marginal tax rates above 25 percent, which applied to taxable incomes above $12,900 for unmarried individuals and $20,000 for joint returns, accounted for only 13 percent of total income tax revenues.[14] That is all that would be lost if taxpayers reported exactly the same taxable income as they did in 1977, but that would not have happened. If the maximum rate were only 25 percent, it would no longer be prof-

[14] Milton Friedman, "A Simple Tax Reform," *Newsweek*, August 18, 1980, p. 68.

itable to pay the thirty, forty, or fifty cents per dollar that many now sacrifice in order to take advantage of tax shelters. Those shelters are expensive because they often yield low before-tax rates of return relative to risk, and syndication, accounting, and legal fees can be enormous. Consequently, a lower tax rate would diminish the use of shelters, and taxable income would rise even if total economic activity remained constant. In order to keep tax revenue constant, the taxable income of 1977 taxpayers above the 25 percent bracket would have to rise by less than 20 percent, and such an increase is highly plausible.

Friedman notes that in 1929 the top marginal rate was 24 percent, levied on net taxable income above $100,000. Almost 15,000 reported such an income. Given population and income growth between 1929 and 1977, there should have been 27,000 returns reporting taxable income greater than $1 million in 1977. In fact, only 1,785 returns reported adjusted gross income above this figure. Data on taxable income are not published, but clearly, fewer than 1,785 would have had taxable incomes above $1 million.[15]

Given that the tax law is now riddled with many more loopholes than existed in 1929, some would continue to be used even if all rates above 25 percent were reduced to that level. Therefore, we could not expect the number of returns reporting more than $1 million in taxable income to rise fifteenfold. Friedman's analysis clearly indicates, however, that rates above 25 percent serve no useful purpose. It is very likely that tax receipts would increase if such tax rates were lowered, and even if receipts did not actually rise, revenue losses are sure to be trivial. Meanwhile, a huge deadweight loss could be eliminated. Many syndicators, accountants, and lawyers could turn their talents to socially productive occupations, and the efficiency of the allocation of work effort and savings would rise significantly.

Many of the arguments in support of progressive taxes have been examined closely in recent years and have been found wanting. Evidence shows that progressive taxes have distorted the economy's ability to allocate resources efficiently and have created

[15] Ibid. Arthur Laffer has popularized the view that there may be a more general inverse relation between tax rates and tax revenues. For a discussion of this proposition, see "Two Views of the Kemp-Roth Bill," *AEI Economist* (July 1978).

measurable disincentives to work and investment. In academic circles, a review of the literature suggests that the proponents of progressive taxes are now on the defensive. Proponents now base their support of the system largely on ethics and political realities, admitting that neither "rational arguments" nor "empirical inquiry," according to James Tobin, a prominent liberal economist, will satisfactorily resolve the issue.[16] He concludes, as did Henry Simon many years ago, that "the case for drastic progression in taxation must be rested on the case against inequality—on the ethical or aesthetic judgment that the prevailing distribution of wealth and income reveals a degree (and/or kind) of inequality that is distinctly evil or unlovely."[17]

Aesthetics, however, is a matter of subjective judgment and of opinion, and ethics even more so. Steep progressive taxes may raise uncomfortable ethical questions of confiscation and extreme interference with personal liberty if one chooses to look at democratically determined redistribution schemes in this way. Anyone who embraces democratic principles may also believe that democratically determined objectives do not justify trampling on basic human rights and liberties. A case can be made that a right to the fruits of one's labor, or a reasonable approximation thereof, is clearly in the realm of natural rights and liberties: it is not something to be trifled with casually when it poses an obstacle to some immediate social objective.

These arguments, of course, do not settle the issue; they merely raise other fundamental principles, which have equal ethical validity. When the issue of progressivity is reduced to ethics and aesthetics, the case is still weak or, to quote Blum and Kalven, "uneasy."[18] Obviously, philosophical arguments will not necessarily convince people that progressivity should be lessened. But there are also many practical problems caused by progressivity, which have to be faced regardless of a person's philosophy.

[16] James Tobin, "Considerations Regarding Taxation and Inequality," in Colin D. Campbell ed., *Income Redistribution* (Washington, D.C.: American Enterprise Institute, 1977), p. 127.

[17] Henry Simons, *Personal Income Taxation* (Chicago: University of Chicago Press, 1938), pp. 18–19.

[18] Walter J. Blum and Harry Kalven, Jr., *The Uneasy Case for Progressive Taxation* (Chicago: University of Chicago Press, 1953).

This brings us to what I consider to be the issue of overriding importance, the effect of a progressive tax structure on work and investment incentives, an issue that until recently was casually dismissed by policy makers and economists as insignificant. This view is changing. Intuitively, one would expect that the suppliers of labor would be more willing to work as wages rose. The same should hold for capital. Conversely, any reduction in wages or profits ought to diminish the supply of these goods and services and, hence, total output. Any tax, of course, reduces one's net earnings and should, therefore, reduce the work incentive. Progressive tax rates exacerbate this effect because they work at the margin. The incremental amount of labor bears the greatest tax, and thus these incremental efforts receive the greatest discouragement. In other words, beyond some minimum amount of labor, the net reward for extra amounts offered actually declines.

While it seems clear that such a perverse reward system ought to discourage work, a casual impression of human behavior might suggest that the effect is trivial. After all, the number of hours worked per week has declined over time even though after-tax wages have risen. Economic theory does suggest that—all else equal—people will choose more leisure as living standards improve. Moreover, most employment contracts are for a fixed workweek, typically forty hours, and employees do not have the option of reducing it within the structure of the organized work place. Although adjustments to this work standard are not easy to make, there is a recent trend in labor contracts among highly paid workers toward greater amounts of paid time off. Since paid vacations are an explicit cost to the firm (other workers must be hired as replacements), there may be no difference to the company between an increase in pay and an increase in vacation time. The worker may choose more time off because the higher marginal tax rates on extra wages make them less desirable.

For workers who do not have bargaining strengths that permit extensive nontaxable forms of compensation, there are other ways in which labor can be withheld. High marginal tax rates discourage workers from taking part-time jobs to supplement household incomes; so instead of extra work and extra income they decide in favor of leisure. The reader may think that this problem is insignificant because high marginal rates affect only the rich, who are a small portion of the labor force. A recently published review of the current tax issues, however, showed that the combination of federal and state income taxes and payroll taxes (social security) results in a marginal tax rate of 43 percent for a married resident of Massachusetts earning only $12,000 per year.[19] Such a person must pay nearly half of any extra earnings to government, a strong disincentive to enhancing his or her material well-being by working extra hours.

The trend toward using free time to engage in economically productive activities that are not subject to taxation is related to the preference for more time off. With a 43 percent marginal tax rate, a family must earn $1,754 before taxes to be able to pay $1,000 to have their house painted. If the painter also faces a 43 percent marginal tax rate, he nets only $570. Because the benefits of working on one's home are not taxed, the family could, in effect, "earn" $1,000 by using their free time to do a paint job that would net the expert only $570. Superficially, it would appear that this redirection of labor is not undesirable because useful work is still being performed. While this is partly true, such a redirection represents an inefficient do-it-yourself activity, which results in a lower total output. Society loses the benefits of specialization and division of labor, which have been so important to modern economic growth and greater labor productivity. It is not surprising that underground economic activity is taking place in this area of personal services.

High marginal tax rates also discourage spouses from entering the work force. Since the system taxes family rather than individual incomes, most of the second worker's income is taxed at rates that begin at the marginal rate applied to the primary worker's income. This results in a take-home pay for the second worker that is below that of a single person holding the same job. In the case of the hypothetical Massachusetts family, the initial tax rate for the second worker would begin at a very high level. Such a system discourages households from improving their standard of living and, by discouraging wives from working, diminishes the wealth of the nation by idling productive resources.

[19] Martin Feldstein, "The Tax Revolt and Future Tax Legislation," *The Data Resources Review of the U.S. Economy*, vol. 8, no. 12 (December 1978), pp. 1.19–1.25.

While anecdotal evidence supports the view that high taxes reduce the amount of labor offered by individuals, the empirical evidence on the issue is, at best, mixed. Statistical studies have failed to establish a definite negative relationship between taxes and labor supply.[20] The effect of rising taxes on leisure is difficult to isolate when real income, which also affects leisure, has been rising during the period under study. Future improvements in data collection and statistical analysis will, one hopes, eliminate the ambiguity which now clouds the issue.

Any study which confines itself solely to examining the effect of high marginal tax rates on the number of hours worked misses another important component of the issue. It says nothing about how hard people work while they are on the job. Workers clearly have less incentive to break their backs to get a raise or a promotion if their new higher income puts them into a higher tax bracket.

High marginal tax rates also discourage savings. Any return to added savings will be taxed at a person's highest marginal rate and, especially in an inflationary era, this can be devastating. Imagine a person saving in a passbook savings account paying a return of 5.5 percent. A 25 percent marginal tax bracket reduces the return to 4.1 percent. With an inflation rate of 10 percent, the value of the person's savings is eroding in real terms at a rate greater than 5 percent per year. Even a corporate bond yielding 13 percent does not provide much solace. A 25 percent tax rate reduces the net yield to about 9.75 percent. The person's saving still yields a negative rate of return with a 10 percent inflation rate.

It is little wonder that, in a desperate attempt to protect themselves against inflation, people are fleeing from bonds and savings accounts into real estate, antiques, paintings, and coins. Such behavior, though clearly understandable, reduces productive busi-

[20] The debate on this subject is extensive and active. There is agreement that taxes decrease the labor supply of "secondary workers" such as teenagers. The main question is on the effects on labor supplied by prime-aged males. See Cain and Watts, *Income Maintenance and Labor Supply*; Marvin Kosters, "Effects of an Income Tax on Labor Supply," in Arnold Harberger and Martin J. Bailey, eds., *The Taxation of Income from Capital* (Brookings Institution, 1969); Jerry Houseman, "Supply Responses to Changes in Taxation" (Paper presented at a Brookings Institution conference entitled "The Effects of Taxes on Labor Supply," October 1979); and Congressional Budget Office, *An Analysis of the Roth-Kemp Tax Cut Proposal*, 1978, pp. 11–16.

ness investment and so reduces long-run growth and future living standards.

Of course, there are some who value egalitarianism for its own sake and who would continue to argue that it is worth slowing the rate of growth of the economy in order to reduce income disparities. When philosophical views of this type are strongly held, it is often hard to change them with logical argument.

I have argued that the case for egalitarianism is also a case for the confiscation of the fruits of a person's own labors and is, therefore, completely at odds with the fundamental values of the founders of our nation. Even if this view is not accepted, it is clear to me that the pursuit of egalitarianism comes at a very high cost to economic growth. More equality may be attainable, but only at very low living standards for all.

But perhaps the most important point of all is that our current tax system redistributes precious little income. Our highest marginal tax rates raise very little revenue while imposing enormous losses on our economy.

4

Proposals to Reform the Tax System

My desire to moderate the degree of progressivity in the tax system is a useful starting point for discussing comprehensive reform of the tax system. The attainment of my other objectives—simplicity, horizontal equity, and economic efficiency—would, of necessity, entail the elimination of many of the special preferences and deductions that are now available to taxpayers. Without some reduction in marginal tax rates, these reform proposals could be seen as nothing more than an increase in taxes. This is not what is intended. In achieving these objectives, many deductions and loopholes will be removed; but the corresponding reduction in applicable tax rates will, on average, offset them within each income class. Some individual taxpayers will, of course, lose, at least in the short run; we cannot all be winners in the narrow sense of the term, in creating a system that is less complex, economically efficient, and equitable. When considering each of my proposed reforms, readers must bear in mind that, as deductions are lost and income that was formerly free of taxation becomes taxable, the tax rate applied to their individual income will be much lower than at present. As will be demonstrated later, a new, lower rate structure can be implemented, and it will leave the total tax obligation for each income class roughly the same as it is at present.

The starting point for any reform of the tax system must be to clean up and redefine the income base that is to be taxed. Tax experts have given us many choices, each with its own advantages and disadvantages. When I was secretary of the Treasury, I asked my staff to prepare the report *Blueprints for Basic Tax Reform*, an excellent analysis that has become a classic in the field of public finance. Following that report, I will consider two of the major income bases—the comprehensive income base, and the consumption or cash-flow income base. They possess many of the desired reform characteristics, as well as a few problems vis-à-vis each other. But each is clearly superior to the existing system in simplicity, equity, and economic efficiency.

Comprehensive Income Base

Proponents of a comprehensive income tax argue that income should serve as the tax base, because income is a good indicator of the well-being of the tax-paying unit, be it a single individual or a family. By income they mean any inflow to the taxpayer that can be used for consumption or net savings. Any capital gain or asset sale would count as taxable income since it can be either used for consumption or added to saving. But only real capital gains would be taxed since the cost of assets used for tax purposes would be raised each year to take account of inflation.

In-kind income creates special problems, which are considered in the appendix.

That leaves many inflows that are not now taxed, but would have to be under a truly comprehensive income tax base. All transfer payments, such as unemployment insurance, social security, and supplementary security income, would be added to the tax base. At first sight, this would seem to harm many in unfortunate economic circumstances, but the provision of generous exemption levels can take care of this problem, and it must always be remembered that, with a more comprehensive tax base, marginal tax rates would be lowered for all.

Under a true comprehensive income tax, most itemized deductions would disappear, although it may be necessary to compromise in a few areas such as those involving charities and medical expenses. Business would lose special investment incentives such as the investment credit and excess depreciation for subsidized housing. Depreciation deductions and mineral depletion allowances would be adjusted for inflation and designed to reflect, as closely as possible, true economic depreciation and depletion.

The intent is to define capital income properly, so that all investments paying the same economic rate of return are treated equally by the tax system. Then, investment dollars will flow to those areas in which they are most productive. Thus we would eliminate the grossly inefficient misallocation of capital resources that occurs in the present system, where the pattern of investments is determined as much by anomalies in the tax law as by their true productivity.

Of course, there is no role for a corporate income tax in a true comprehensive income tax system. It is obviously absurd to impose a special tax on a business just because its legal form differs from that of an individual proprietorship or a partnership. Ideally, the corporate tax should be completely integrated with the personal tax; that is to say, a dollar of income should be taxed exactly the same way whether it flows through a corporation or through a partnership. There are some technical problems with this that are discussed in the appendix, but in the abstract, integration would work as follows.

All corporate profits would be allocated to the shareholders. This is obviously a simple matter with dividends, but reinvested profits would also have to be allocated, and personal taxes would have to be paid on them. If that were the end of it, a taxpayer would still be taxed twice—once when profits were reinvested on his behalf and again when reinvested profits were reflected in any capital gains on sales of stock. To avoid this, the shareholder's share of reinvested earnings would be added to the cost basis of his shares. For example, every year a shareholder would receive a report from the corporation which said something like, "Your share of the corporation's profits this year was $4,000. That amount should be added to your taxable income. Dividends amounted to $1,000, and $3,000 was reinvested on your behalf. The latter amount should be added to the cost basis of your shares for the purpose of computing any capital gain." If the shareholder had originally paid $20,000 for his shares, capital gains taxes would now be paid only on the amount by which the sales price exceeded $23,000 plus any adjustment for inflation. If the corporation suffered a loss, that loss would also be allocated to the shareholder.

In the example above, the shareholder had to add $4,000 to taxable income even though only $1,000 was paid in dividends.

Since the $4,000 was free of any corporate tax, the shareholder would clearly be better off in the long run than under current tax law, but in the short run a liquidity problem might arise if the marginal personal tax rate exceeded 25 percent. The shareholder would then owe more to the government than was received in dividends. This problem is easily solved by imposing a withholding tax on the corporation. Say the withholding rate was set at 30 percent. The corporation would pay $1,200 to the government on behalf of the taxpayer, reflecting his $4,000 profit share. This amount would be deducted from the shareholder's tax liability to the Treasury just as taxes withheld from wages are now deducted when individual returns are filed in April. To the extent the withholding exceeded the shareholder's tax liability on his share of the profits, the excess would reduce other tax payments or be refunded.

All of this sounds quite complicated, and it is. Much of this complexity could be avoided under the cash-flow tax, which will be described later, and that is one reason I favor the consumption or cash-flow approach.

A comprehensive income tax would, however, be very much simpler than the current system because of the elimination of so many deductions and exclusions. Moreover, the lower marginal rates made possible by a comprehensive income tax would make it much less worthwhile for the taxpayer to expend so much effort looking for every last possible tax advantage even if a few inadvertent loopholes remained.

In the comprehensive tax system described by the *Blueprints*, the top rate would be only 38 percent, which would apply to taxable incomes greater than $40,000. There would be only two other tax brackets: an 8 percent tax rate on incomes from $0 to $4,600 and a 25 percent rate on incomes from $4,600 to $40,000.[21] With a personal exemption of $1,000 and an additional exemption of $1,600 per return, the structure would raise about the same income in 1977 as the law then in effect and would not greatly affect the distribution of the tax burden among income classes.[22] I would, of course, prefer a somewhat less progressive structure, but that could easily be arranged. Any rate structure that was

[21] Treasury Department, *Blueprints*, p. 162.
[22] Treasury Department, *Blueprints*, p. 20, table 1.

adopted would also have to be adjusted for inflation every year to avoid the present problem of bracket creep.

The top marginal rate in the tax structure advocated by the *Blueprints* is higher than the top marginal rate of 25 percent advocated in the previously discussed analysis by Milton Friedman. That result occurs because Friedman implicitly assumes the continuation of the marginal rates now found at the bottom of our current tax rate structure. The *Blueprints* lowers these bottom rates while expanding the tax base. It is, in my view, highly probable that if the *Blueprint* reforms were actually implemented, the improvement in economic efficiency and in tax compliance would be so substantial that current revenues could in fact be raised with lower marginal rates than were computed in that volume.

Although a comprehensive income tax system would clearly be vastly superior to our present mess, it is not free of problems. I have described only some of the complexities related to corporate tax integration. More are described in the appendix. I have quickly passed over the problem of adjusting capital gains, depreciation deductions and depletion allowances, and other items for inflation, but such adjustments make tax returns very complicated.

Further, the system still creates disincentives for savings. The disincentive is much less than under the present system because the removal of the corporate tax would cause corporations to flourish and the top personal rate would be lowered from 70 percent to, at most, 38 percent.[23] Returns to savings would still be reduced by the tax system, however, and to solve that problem we must turn to the consumption or cash-flow tax.

Consumption or Cash-Flow Tax

There are both profound philosophical and practical reasons for favoring a consumption tax over an income tax. The philosophical argument has been around for more than two hundred years. Thomas Hobbes argued that it was much more equitable to tax a person on what was withdrawn from society as roughly measured by the taxpayer's consumption than on what was contributed to society as roughly measured by the taxpayer's income.

It can be argued further that a person's consumption is a better indicator of well-being than income. A person's ability to

[23] Treasury Department, *Blueprints*, p. 162.

consume is determined by both income and wealth and differs according to whether income is constant and relatively certain or highly irregular and uncertain. Consumption tends to be much smoother than income and therefore can be considered a much better index of "ability to pay." Put another way, shouldn't a person's ability and duty to pay for government services be related to the amount he or she decides to consume privately?

As a practical matter, a consumption tax is much simpler than a comprehensive income tax. If you do not tax savings, you do not have to worry about attributing a corporation's reinvested profits to shareholders. Moreover, you do away with all of the problems related to measuring capital income in an inflationary era. Indexing capital gains, depreciation, debt, and the like is not necessary if capital income is not taxed. Even if one does not accept any of the philosophical arguments for consumption taxation, the practical arguments are, in my view, overwhelming.

And, of course, there is no disincentive to savings. Capital formation and, therefore, economic growth are enhanced, leading to better living standards for all.

Many object to consumption taxes because they misunderstand the basic concept. They believe the poor would be badly hurt because they tend to consume a high proportion of their income. (In fact, the portion often exceeds 100 percent for brief periods.)

A consumption tax can be as progressive as society may desire. In fact, tax returns could be designed to look very much as they would under a comprehensive income tax. It was previously noted that income can be comprehensively defined to equal consumption plus net savings. Under a consumption tax, the taxpayer could simply compute income and deduct savings. The residual equals consumption, and a progressive rate structure can be applied to this amount.

But if this approach is followed, all of the previously mentioned complexities associated with defining comprehensive income arise. Therefore, the *Blueprints* favors a so-called cash-flow approach, which provides a much simpler method of computing total consumption.

Under this approach (with a few exceptions noted in the appendix), all cash inflows to the tax unit would be added up.

This would include the proceeds from sale of assets, withdrawals from bank accounts, wages, dividends, interest, and rent. All cash outflows used to purchase assets, like stocks, bonds, and savings accounts, would then be deducted. Obviously, the residual, which is the cash inflow not used to accumulate assets, must be consumption.

The net result of all of this is that any income that is saved escapes taxation and the after-tax return to saving becomes equal to the before-tax return. Thus, there is no disincentive to saving. This can be illustrated by the following example. Suppose that a taxpayer in a 30 percent tax bracket decides to buy $10,000 worth of corporate bonds paying 10 percent interest. Because this purchase is deducted from the tax base, it costs the taxpayer $7,000 after taxes. If after a year the bond is sold to finance some consumption, the taxpayer will have to add $11,000 ($10,000 in principle plus, assuming that interest rates remain constant, $1,000 in interest) to his or her tax base. Because the whole amount is now subject to taxation, a 30 percent tax will have to be paid, leaving $7,700 for consumption. Since the after-tax cost was originally $7,000, the taxpayer has still earned 10 percent on his saving after taxes—the same as the before-tax rate of return.

Note that our current tax system already has many of the features of a cash-flow system. Within prescribed limits pension savings are now deductible from the tax base, but a tax has to be paid when the savings are withdrawn upon retiring. Capital gains taxes are not levied on the sale of owner-occupied housing if the proceeds are reinvested in another house. Under a pure cash-flow tax, no tax would be levied as long as the proceeds were rolled over into any investment. It would not have to be another house. Under the cash-flow tax system described in the *Blueprints*, there would be an exemption of $1,500 per return and an exemption of $800 per person. The tax rates would be 10 percent on consumption in excess of the exemptions of $0 to $5,200; 28 percent on $5,201 to $30,000; and 40 percent on consumption above $30,000.[24]

Some worry that a consumption tax system would allow some families to accumulate great wealth. First, it should be noted that any gift or inheritance used to finance consumption would, of course, be taxed. To the extent that successive generations of

[24] Treasury Department, *Blueprints*, p. 169.

particular families save this money, I perceive that as a social gain rather than as a problem, but for practical political reasons it may be necessary to supplement a consumption tax system with a special tax levied on funds transferred through gifts or inheritances.

Of course, any tax system will have to deal with some complex tax issues, and such matters are discussed in the appendix. A reader who persists that far will find that the list of problems is quite substantial. But compared with our present tax system, a cash-flow tax is the essence of simplicity. Under it, we could dispense with the pages of law and volumes of regulation which deal with matters such as differentiating capital gains from regular income, recapturing depreciation, ensuring that corporations are not formed solely to shelter income, stock options, differing depletion allowances, and so on and on.

In addition to making great strides toward simplicity, the enormous efficiency gain stemming from the cash-flow proposal must be reemphasized. Savings would be greatly enhanced. There would no longer be any discrimination against corporate investment because there would be no corporate tax. More generally, savings would flow to those investments that are most productive to the economy as a whole because all returns to capital would be taxed at a zero rate, and there would no longer be the great array of differing tax provisions, which now attempt to push capital here, there, and everywhere.

I think it clear that the whole society would be better off in the longer run. I cannot claim, however, that no one would be hurt in the short run. Under our current unwieldy system some people escape taxation altogether. Some of these are very rich while others are toward the lower end of the income distribution. Under my proposal the poorest of the poor would be protected from taxes by the exemptions, but otherwise anyone who consumed goods and services would be taxed. That would include people of modest income who now live on transfer payments. But if consumption is modest, the tax burden would also be modest because the proposal implies such low marginal tax rates.

I believe strongly that the current tax system has exempted too large a portion of the population from federal tax obligations. If a large part of the population does all of the receiving while the rest does all of the giving, divisiveness can be the only result. Politicians can build a career by pandering to the recipient classes, and the whole basis of our democracy becomes unstable.

In recent years, all reform proposals and new programs, regardless of their primary intent, have had to contain clearly identifiable benefits that accrue to all classes of society, and no one should ever suffer any pain. Programs established to solve, for instance, some particular urban problem are often modified to incorporate benefits for suburbs and rural areas so that everybody can get "a piece of the action." The energy issue is another case in point. Despite the mounting problems arising from excessive consumption and shrinking supply, progress toward energy price decontrol is stymied by claims that the poor would be hurt, even though great benefits would accrue to society as a whole. Such problems may be typical of the compromise and consensus building inherent in a democratic system, requiring majority support for any major initiative. Sometimes, however, reform is held hostage to promote unrelated objectives, in acts of flagrant self-interest.

Examples of such shortsightedness abound. Rent controls are passed, allegedly to protect the poor, but end up reducing the stock of rental housing to the point that the poor suffer. Minimum wage laws are sold the same way, but often leave the young and unskilled with no jobs at all. Similarly, usury ceilings do nothing but leave certain activities with no source of credit in periods of generally high interest rates.

In summary, it would be the height of foolishness to reject a sensible tax reform proposal just because not everyone can benefit in the very short run. If we try to protect everyone, all will eventually suffer since there will be no hope of ever reversing the present disastrous course of our economy.

5

The Experiences of Other Industrialized Nations

Having begun the paper with a number of striking comparisons between the economic performance of the United States and that of its trading partners, it is only fitting that we should close by comparing the tax treatment of capital income in those nations with tax treatment in the United States. Such a comparison offers useful instruction on two important points. First, most of the major industrial powers offer extensive tax concessions on capital income. They are well ahead of the United States in perceiving the need for a tax system that encourages both savings and investment. Some tax capital gains on security sales at low rates if at all. Many provide special incentives to savers. In other words, they have moved a long way toward the philosophy embodied in my consumption or cash-flow tax proposal. They have done this because they recognize the importance of capital formation. In my view, it is no accident that they have done better than the United States. Their successes are, in large part, the result of tax systems that reduce disincentives toward capital formation.

We must, of course, remain vigilant on the spending side of the budget as well. A Hudson Institute study of advanced industrial countries indicated that the higher the share of government in a country's GNP, the more likely the country would grow more slowly.[25]

[25] "Government Growth Crowds Out Investment," *Business Week*, October 18, 1976, pp. 138–39.

But returning to the main point of this study, it must be noted that the United States has fewer tax concessions to individual savers and investors than any of its major trading partners has. Most of the advanced industrialized nations use their tax systems to encourage savings over consumption. While the heavy reliance by the European countries on the value-added tax is the best example of this preference, their personal income tax systems also include numerous incentives that relate directly to savings. Several of them resemble elements of the proposed consumption-base tax.

The Japanese, whose savings as a percentage of after-tax income are slightly more than 20 percent (compared with an average of slightly more than 6 percent in the United States during the 1970s), have a wide variety of incentives for savers. Capital gains on security sales are generally exempt from taxes. A portion of life insurance premiums is deductible. The interest on up to $12,000 in a personal savings account with the post office (a major savings institution in Japan) is exempt from income taxes, as is interest on government bonds up to the same amount. Interest on savings of up to $20,000 with one's employer is also exempt.

Dividends from one company up to a certain maximum are subject to only a 20 percent withholding tax. A person with an income below $40,000 is allowed an income tax credit equal to 10 percent of his dividends. Above $40,000, the credit drops to 5 percent. For savings accounts set up for the purchase of a house, a person is entitled to a tax credit equal to 8 percent of net savings, up to a certain maximum per year.

Germany has not only tax incentives for saving but also a number of cash bonus arrangements. A married couple with a household income of up to $24,000 can receive a tax-free cash grant from the government equal to 14 percent of the amount invested in securities through special accounts. The government pays an additional 2 percent for each dependent child. The maximum amount of the grant is approximately $800. These special accounts must be blocked for six to seven years, and the cash grant is credited directly to the account. Such cash grants are also available for net additions to savings accounts at the same rate and with the same limitations.

For savings in a building and loan association, a person is allowed to deduct from his taxable income 50 percent of his mean annual savings during the first four years of the account. Employees are also permitted to invest in an employer-sponsored investment plan and to receive a tax-free grant of 30 percent of the amount invested up to a specified maximum. The grant rises to 40 percent if the employee has three or more children. As in Japan, gains on the sale of securities are generally exempt from taxation, as is a portion of the life insurance premium.

In France, a withholding tax system on interest earnings limits the maximum tax rate on such earnings to 33⅓ percent. On dividends received, a person is permitted a tax credit equal to 50 percent of the amount of the dividend. On the sale of securities, one-half of the capital gain is exempt from taxation after adjustment for inflation.

Canada expands on the present U.S. practice of exempting the first $100 of dividends from taxation by exempting the first $1,000 of interest, dividends, and capital gains. Further, a tax credit equal to one-half of dividends received is allowed, and the income is then "grossed up" to include the dividend plus one-half the allowable credit. Contributions of up to $1,000 per year to a homeownership savings plan are deductible, a feature similar to the consumption-base plan. The withdrawal is nontaxable if used for the purchase of a home.

Italy generally excludes capital gains from taxable income and permits shareholders a tax credit equal to one-third of the dividends received. Tax-withholding arrangements effectively reduce the tax on interest from corporate bonds to either 10 percent or 20 percent, depending on the type of bond, and to 18 percent for interest on savings accounts. Life insurance premiums and contributions to a pension fund are deductible up to a certain maximum.

When these concessions are compared with those available to the U.S. taxpayer, it is painfully obvious how little we do to promote savings. Our new exemption of the first $200 of dividends and interest income, our qualified retirement plans, our limited tax concessions, and our capital gains privileges pale in comparison with the generous incentives offered to the investors of Germany, Japan, and France, which in no small part have contributed to personal savings rates that are more than double ours.

6
A Final Note

The alert reader may recall that the opening paragraph of this book was purposely vague. A turning point, after all, can imply any number of directions. If we see ourselves, as I do, as muddling along on an economic growth path of unimpressive dimensions, a decision can result in an improvement, in more of the same, or in growing weakness. Our situation might best be described by the Chinese character *jiu*, which signifies both danger and opportunity. It sometimes takes a period of serious economic adversity to persuade a nation that fundamental change is needed. The signs of decline have now emerged, painfully so, and only the most hidebound dogmatists could argue that they are not a manifestation of fundamental problems. The problems are correctable, and the proposals offered in this book would help solve them by dramatically altering the way in which we treat people who act in the best interests of the nation. The opportunity exists, but we must act quickly and correctly. To delay needed change makes change much more difficult to implement.

Appendix

No tax system is free of problems. This appendix discusses some of the more interesting technical issues that must be resolved in implementing a comprehensive income tax or a cash-flow tax. Not all such issues are discussed. For a complete discussion the reader is referred to the *Blueprints for Basic Tax Reform*.

A Comprehensive Income Tax

In the text it was noted that comprehensive income can be defined as consumption plus net saving. In a pure system, all in-kind income should be part of the tax base. This would create immense practical difficulties, however.

There are a great variety of in-kind benefits received by individuals and families. Many of our transfer payments take the form of services rather than cash. Employees often receive in-kind services from their employers. Owners of houses and other consumer durables receive a flow of services over time from their investments. A person investing in a house, for example, gains in that he avoids the need to pay rent. An investment in a bond which paid a comparable return would add to taxable income; so when imputed rent is not taxed, the homeowner gains an advantage over investors in other assets.

In most instances it would be practically impossible to value such in-kind benefits. Therefore, it is reasonable to exclude in-kind transfers and imputed rent on houses and other consumer durables from the tax base. The deduction for any property taxes or use taxes on houses and other consumer durables would be disallowed in a comprehensive income tax system, but the mortgage interest and other interest deductions would continue. Otherwise, once imputed rent is exempted, the tax system would discriminate against those who borrow to finance a house or consumer durables and in favor of those who finance the purchase with their own equity. The reason for this is obvious. In a perfect world, a housing investment would be treated like a business. The gross income would consist of imputed rent, and all expenses involved in earning that income—including interest—would be deductible. All other things equal, the person borrowing to finance the housing investment would have a lower net rent income than the one who financed the house out of equity. Therefore, in a perfect system, the mortgage-financed house would add less to taxable income than a house financed entirely with equity. It would not seem equitable to discriminate against mortgage-financed houses just because imputed rent cannot be added to taxable income; therefore, the mortgage interest deduction would continue under a comprehensive income tax. Then, just as under a perfect system, the buyer of a mortgage-financed house would have a lower taxable income than a buyer financing the whole purchase with equity.

A special effort would be made to value in-kind services provided by employers, or else an obvious tax loophole would exist. Medical insurance premiums paid by employers would remain deductible for them but would be added to the taxable income of the employee. Disability benefits would be taxed when received.

Perhaps the most difficult technical problem faced in a comprehensive income tax system involves the complete integration of the corporate and personal income tax. Profits have to be distributed among different classes of shareholders, and some more or less arbitrary rules may have to be developed to do this. Special problems are created by shareholders who sell their stock during the year. The *Blueprints* suggests that the record date be the beginning of the corporate accounting year. That is to say, people buying during the year would not have profits or losses attributed to them until the next year. If the record date were the end of the year, much concentrated trading would result because there would be an incentive for low-bracket taxpayers to sell any losses that emerged to high-bracket taxpayers.

In the text, the integrated system was described as one in

which all reinvested profits are added to the cost basis of shares for the purpose of computing capital gains. The *Blueprints* does things a bit differently. All profits (or losses) are added to (or subtracted from) the cost basis of shares, and dividends are deducted. For people who hold the stock the whole year, this amounts to the same thing as was described in the text, since reinvested profits equal profits minus dividends. The *Blueprints* approach simplifies matters, however, for people who sell during the year. Dividends paid after the record date but before the sale of the stock would be deducted from the cost basis. The sale price would be presumed to reflect any profits reinvested before the sale, and sellers of stock could settle their debt to the tax collector without waiting for a yearend statement from the corporation.

Corporations are often subjected to audits, and profits and tax liabilities for years long past are often altered. It would be too complicated to find and amend the past tax returns of people who had long since sold their shares. Therefore, gains or losses resulting from audits would be allocated to the shareholders of record during the year in which the matter was resolved. In essence, our current tax system does the same thing. It is the current shareholders who suffer if corporations have to pay extra, unanticipated taxes on profits earned in the distant past.

The Consumption or Cash-Flow System

The text described this system as though all savings could easily be deducted from the tax base when they were made. For most savings that is true. A system of "qualified accounts" would be established. Deposits into the accounts would be deductible, and withdrawals would be taxed. Qualified accounts would involve things like bank accounts, stock investments, and pension funds, which are easily traceable. Checking accounts, which yield a constant stream of services, would not be considered qualified accounts.

Occasionally, savings are invested in things that are not typically traded on public exchanges. If, for example, the purchase of a painting or antique were deductible, the IRS might not be able to document the sale of the asset when it was used to finance consumption or used to make a deductible addition to a qualifying account. It might, therefore, be useful not to allow such a purchase to be deducted from the tax base in the year that it was made. In return, any gain on the sale would also be tax-free.

In general, it would be useful to allow a parallel system of qualified and nonqualified accounts to exist, and the taxpayers should be given wide latitude in deciding whether to invest in qualified or nonqualified accounts or to borrow from either qualified or nonqualified lenders. Borrowing from qualified lenders would be added to the tax base while borrowing from nonqualified lenders would not. Then loan repayments to qualified lenders would be deductible while repayments to nonqualified lenders would not.

If the taxpayer is allowed free choice, he can engage in averaging out his tax burden over time when buying costly consumer durables in any one year. For example, imagine a person borrowing $30,000 to purchase a $40,000 house. If he was forced to borrow from a qualified account, the whole $40,000 ($30,000 loan plus $10,000 down payment) would be added to his tax base that year. Mortgage repayments would subsequently be deductible because they are payments to a qualified account. But the tax liability would be enormous in the year in which the home was purchased. Instead, the taxpayer could be allowed to borrow from a nonqualified account. Then the $30,000 mortgage would not be added to taxable income in the year in which the loan was made, and subsequent mortgage payments would not be deductible. That would leave the $10,000 down payment in the tax base, and that is still a large amount. If the home buyer had foresight, however, he could save up for the down payment in a nonqualified account. Payments to that account would not be deductible when made, but the withdrawal of the $10,000 would also escape taxation.

In essence, when a deposit is made in a nonqualified account, taxes on the return are prepaid in that, as in the current system, net savings in nonqualified accounts are made out of after-tax income. But our present tax system again taxes any return to savings. In a consumption system that return would not be taxed.

A parallel system of qualified and nonqualified accounts does create some problems. A huge return to a nonqualified account escapes taxation, and that may bother some people. But huge returns are generally possible only on risky investments, and losses could not be deducted either.

Because a person in effect prepays the tax on deposits in nonqualified accounts, a further problem arises if, before the funds are withdrawn, tax rates rise significantly, say to finance a war. This tax increase is avoided by investing in a nonqualified account, but similarly the investor gains nothing from any subsequent tax reduction.

Transition Problems

Any radical change in tax law involves serious transition problems. Any asset that is taxed less heavily under a new law rises in value while more heavily taxed assets fall in value. The resulting redistribution of wealth may be considered to be inequitable. There are also changes in the timing of tax burdens. Rules have to be established for carrying over old losses or gains and deductions of various types.

The transition to a consumption system is particularly difficult. Almost everyone would have assets that were purchased out of after-tax income under the old law. With a pure consumption tax, sales of such assets should be added to the tax base when the proceeds are used to finance consumption, but this would be quite unfair. On the other hand, gains on such assets should not escape taxation altogether when they are used to finance consumption.

The *Blueprints* develops a number of options for handling such problems. They will not be described here, and the reader is referred to the *Blueprints* for details. It must be noted that all of the options are imperfect and complex. This is unfortunate, but unavoidable. Short-run difficulties should not prevent us, however, from adopting a radical tax reform that will serve us well in the decades ahead.